CHILDREN'S EDUCATIONAL BOOK:

JUNIOR
VINCENT VAN GOGH

D1308778

ISBN-13: 978-1482665536

Cover image: Bedroom in Arles (3rd version) by van Gogh, 1889.

Title image: Self-portrait by van Gogh, 1889.

CONTENTS

There is no letter 'f' at the end of 'van Gogh'.

When you say it, it rhymes with the Scottish word 'loch'.

3

The Church at Auvers (Just north of Paris), 1890

4

INTRODUCTION

Before you read this book I should warn you about two things: firstly that Vincent van Gogh's life has a sad ending and secondly that you may find it impossible to look at his paintings and not want to go straight off and do some painting yourself. If you get this feeling you are not alone. Van Gogh's broad and colourful brushstrokes, and his beautiful patterned paintings have **inspired** (in-spy-erd) many artists. (If you are inspired it means something has made you want to have a go).

If I had to choose one word to describe Vincent van Gogh it would be **passionate** (pash-on-at) which means to care deeply about something. Whatever mood he was in he was passionately in that mood. If he was feeling angry he would be very angry (so angry in fact that he once cut part of his ear off after an argument with another artist. You can see the bandage in this famous self-portrait). When he was unhappy he felt *so* lost and unloved that sometimes he had to go into hospital for his own safety.

Self-portrait with a Bandaged Ear, 1889

5

We can't be sure of what illness van Gogh was suffering from. Modern doctors have come up with different suggestions but it was probably some kind of **mental illness**. 'Mental' means 'to do with the mind' and the brain, just like any other part of the body, can sometimes be ill. It wasn't van Gogh's fault. He couldn't help it, it was probably something he was born with, although his lifestyle of drinking too much alcohol didn't help his condition.

This may all seem a very gloomy way to start a book, but van Gogh's passion had its upside. When he was feeling happy he wasn't just content, he was brimming with excitement and so bubbling with ideas that he just couldn't stop himself from painting. It was when he was in these moods that his great artistic genius shone.

PAINTING STYLE

Van Gogh was one of the first artists to use a style called **Expressionism** (Ex-presh-on-ism). Instead of painting the colours that he actually saw, he painted any colour he felt like, according to his mood. He used colours to *express* himself. For example, he wanted this painting of a night café to be a seedy bar filled with shifty unpleasant characters, so he purposely painted the walls blood red to make it feel like "the devil's furnace". This use of expressionism means that many of van Gogh's most famous paintings are very colourful, but it wasn't always that way. As we'll see, in his early years his paintings were quite dark with only splashes of light.

The Night Cafe, 1888

7

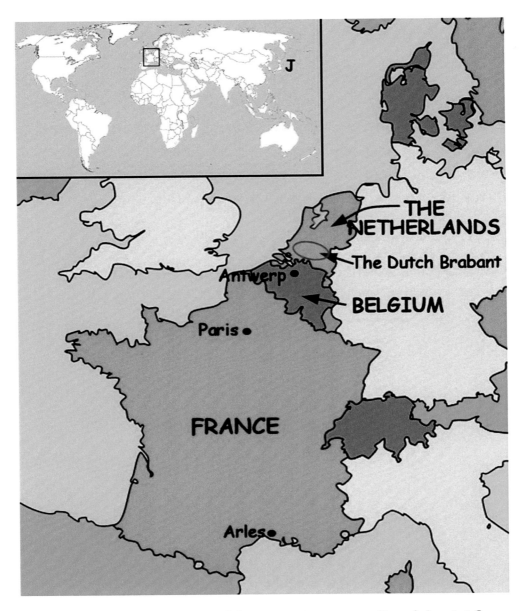

Some Important Places in van Gogh's Life

EARLY YEARS

Van Gogh was a quiet child with bright blue/green eyes and ginger hair. He was born just over 150 years ago in 1853. His parents lived in The Netherlands, close to the border with Belgium. People from The Netherlands are **Dutch** and this area of the country is called the Dutch Brabant.

Then, like now, the Dutch Brabant was mostly countryside full of farms. The people who worked hard all day on the farms were called **peasants** (pe-zants). Many artists in the past had painted peasants at work looking as if they were content and happy with their lot. These artists had a very **romantic** (row-man-tic) picture of the peasants' lives (they liked to think it was a fairy tale life). Van Gogh could see that the truth was very different. He could see that the peasants were not happy; they worked *too* hard and did not have enough to eat. He felt great **sympathy** (sim-path-ee) for them (he understood how they

were really feeling because he too knew what it felt like to be very unhappy) and he even once gave all his belongings to some of them. So when van Gogh painted the peasants he painted the reality of how they lived—whenever an artist does this we call it **Realism** (Real-ism).

Peasant Sitting by the Fireplace ('Worn Out'), 1881

Who Inspired van Gogh?

Artists are often inspired by the painters who have come before them and van Gogh was no different. One of the first painters that van Gogh liked was **Rembrandt** (Rem-brant)**,** also a Dutchman, who had lived in the 17th century (the sixteen hundreds). Rembrandt painted a lot of portraits of people and his Art is also a good example of Realism. This is a painting by Rembrandt—how do you think the girl is feeling? Van Gogh also liked the way Rembrandt painted bright highlights on a very dark background.

A Girl with a Broom by Rembrandt, 1651

When van Gogh painted the peasants in the Dutch Brabant he painted them without much colour but with strong lights on a very dark background just as Rembrandt had. Van Gogh's most famous painting of the peasants is the following one, called 'The Potato Eaters'. You can see how thin and unhappy the people look. Look at their hands, they are all skin and bone.

The Potato Eaters, 1885

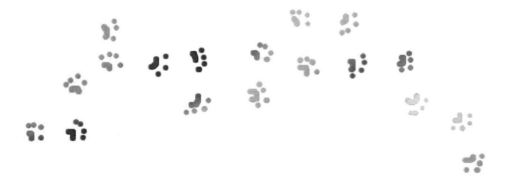

11

ART SCHOOL

You may be surprised to hear that during those early years van Gogh was not a **professional** (pro-fesh-on-al) artist (he didn't paint to earn his money). At that time he was very religious (though later he stopped believing in God) and for some of it he was a preacher, like his father. He also worked for an Art dealer (a company that sells paintings) and in a book shop.

The Courtesan, 1887

1885 (Moved to Paris)
-1853 (Born)
32

Finally in 1885, when he was 32 years old, van Gogh decided to train to be an artist. First he studied in Antwerp in Belgium and then in Paris, the capital city of France, where he lived with his brother Theo for a while. Paris in the 1880's was *the* place to be if you were an artist and van Gogh felt like he had had a new lease of life. He met other artists and they discussed the latest Art, like the Japanese style which you can see in this painting (Japan is marked with a letter 'J' on the world map on pg 8). They held shows and thought about nothing but Art. During the two years he was living there van Gogh painted 200 paintings. It was in Paris that he decided to start using more colours.

12

A MASTER AT WORK

Van Gogh worked hard and played hard in Paris and he soon grew tired and unwell from smoking and drinking too much, so he moved to the warmth of a place called Arles in the south of France. He wanted to go somewhere where there was bright sunshine to suit his colourful **palette** (pal-et). A palette is the board that artists mix paint on, like the one on the title page of this book, but we often use the word more broadly to mean the range of colours that an artist chooses. Van Gogh wanted to start an artists' community in Arles.

The move was a good decision because it was here that he painted some of his best paintings, including his most famous ones of sunflowers.

Sunflowers, 1888

13

Van Gogh liked to use colours from the opposite sides of the colour wheel together in the same picture. We call these **complementary** (com-pli-ment-ary) colours. He often painted blues next to oranges and yellows as you can see in the next two paintings. One is of the house he lived in in Arles and the other is of some tired peasants resting under a haystack in a wheat field. (Van Gogh painted a lot of wheat fields).

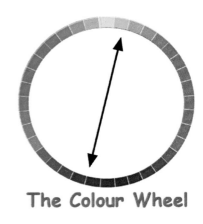

The Colour Wheel

Noon, Rest from Work, 1890

14

The Yellow House, 1888

A **succession** (suc-sesh-on) of artists (one after the other) did join van Gogh in Arles, including **Paul Gauguin** (Go-gan) who painted him while he was painting the sunflowers. Unfortunately van Gogh was not an easy person to get along with and none of them stayed very long. After arguing with Gauguin, van Gogh went into hospital again. At first one near Arles but later he moved to one nearer to Theo.

Van Gogh Painting Sunflowers by Paul Gauguin, 1888

Blossoming Almond Tree, 1890

While he was in hospital van Gogh still had periods when he was inspired to paint and he continued to work on some more of his most famous paintings, including a tree full of blossom which he painted for the bedroom of his new nephew, Theo's son Vincent Willem.

16

Not only did van Gogh continue to paint but his Art finally started to get noticed and he was invited to take part in some important shows. He began to paint the swirling, curling patterns in the backgrounds of his paintings for which he so famous. You can see them in these next two paintings called 'Wheat Field with Cypresses' and 'The Starry Night' and also in the portrait that I put on the title page of this book. Remember how I talked about 'Expressionism' meaning to paint what you feel like rather than what you actually see in front of you—I've never seen a sky that *actually* looks like either of those in the following paintings, have you? No. So he was painting what he felt like rather than exactly what he saw.

Wheat Field with Cypresses, 1888

Notice the yellow and blue again!

The Starry Night, 1889

A TRAGIC ENDING

One afternoon in the summer of 1890, when he was just 37 years old, van Gogh went for a walk in the countryside and most probably shot himself in the chest. Amazingly the bullet bounced off one of his ribs and he managed to walk home! Theo rushed to his bedside but a day later Vincent died from an infection caused by the wound. In the 70 days before his death he painted a new painting every single day. Afterwards word continued to spread about him, first amongst artists and then beyond, until he finally became known as a great master.

Irises, 1889

It is **ironic** (i-ron-ic, strangely the opposite to what you'd expect) to think that here was a man who sometimes had so little money that he had to choose whether to buy food or paint (he often chose paint which did not help his illness) and now his paintings are amongst the most expensive ever sold—some people have paid millions of dollars just to buy one of them! The painting of the irises on the previous page once sold for $53.9 million. ($ is the symbol for dollars, the money used in The United States of America).

If you had $50 million would you buy one of van Gogh's paintings? If so, which one?

QUIZ

1. What was van Gogh's first name? a) Victor, b) Vincent or c) Willem.

2. Which country was van Gogh born in? a) The Netherlands, b) Belgium or c) Never Never Land.

3. You are a famous Art detective. You discover this little known painting by van Gogh. What facts about it can you use to persuade people that it is really his? (Tip: I can think of five).

Landscape with Wheat Sheaves and Rising Moon, 1889

4. Which words best describe van Gogh's style of art? a) Expressionism, b) Pelmanism and c) Realism.

5. What job did van Gogh's father do? Was he a) a teacher, b) an Art dealer or c) a preacher?

6. Which painting does this detail come from?

7. Tricky question: Which century did van Gogh live in?

21

OTHER BOOKS FROM 'SMART READS FOR KIDS'

An adventure story in a world of magical and mischievous famous Art.

Leo is an ordinary boy who dreams of being an explorer, but when his Grandma gives him a special painting he ends up on a magical and multicultural adventure that is far more than he bargained for.

Join Leo on a quest to find his way home from a very mischievous house with enchanted slides, cheeky squirrels, sneaky swings and slimy snot. In Leo's company you'll discover that at the end of the rainbow there is not only treasure, but the greatest treasure of all.

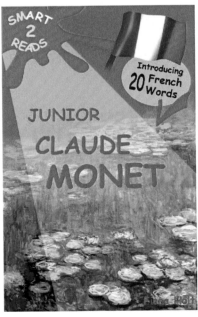

Monet painted over 2000 works during his life. Their titles include useful everyday words such as: Station, Beach, Sea, House and Flowers. They thus provide an excellent and unique opportunity for children to learn some basic French whilst looking at inspiring Art.

Painting selection has been carefully considered. It works chronologically, it includes popular paintings and, crucially, once introduced the title vocabulary reappears later on. So in the latter half of the book children can easily translate titles themselves based on what they have already learned. This reinforces learning by revision, empowering kids with a sense of achievement from the off. It's confidence building, can-do learning.

ANSWERS

1. b) Vincent.

2. a) The Netherlands. (Never Never Land is where Peter Pan lived!)

3.

    i.   The broad brushstrokes.

    ii.   The swirling patterns (especially around the moon, just like in the painting 'The Starry Night').

   iii. The bright colours.

   iv. The use of complementary colours orange and blue together.

    v.   The subject is a wheat field.

4. a) and c) (Pelmanism is the memory game, played with cards, sometimes called Pairs.)

5. c) A preacher.

6. The Night Café on pg 7. Van Gogh often put empty chairs in his paintings. There is also one in the painting on the cover image of this book.

7. The 19th century. (Remember, the century number is always one higher than the first part of the year number, so *1853* was in the *19*th century. If you are six years old this means you have already completed six years of life. All the time that we say you are six years old you are actually part way through your seventh year).

GLOSSARY

Complementary (Com-pli-ment-ary): If two things complement each other they look good, or work well, together. Colours on opposite sides of the colour wheel often look good when put next to each other.

Dutch: Somebody who comes from The Netherlands.

Expressionism (Ex-presh-on-ism): To paint shapes and colours based on how you feel rather than exactly what you see in front of you.

Inspired (In-spy-erd): If something has inspired you it has made you want to have a go.

Ironic (I-ron-ic): Strangely the opposite of what you'd expect.

Mental illness: An illness of the mind.

Palette (Pal-et): A board that artists mix their paints on. Also the range of colours than an artist chooses to use.

Paul Gauguin (Go-gan): A French artist who stayed with van Gogh in Arles for a while.

Passionate (Pash-on-at): To care deeply about something.

Peasant (Pe-zant): People who work hard in the fields for very little money.

Professional (Pro-fesh-on-al): If you are a professional at something you do it to earn your living.

Realism (Real-ism): To paint things and people the way they really are.

Rembrandt (Rem-brant): A Dutch portrait artist who lived in the 17th Century.

Romantic (Row-man-tic): To think that things are all wonderful and perfect, like in a fairy tale.

Succession (Suc-sesh-on): One after the other.

Sympathy (Sim-path-ee): To understand how someone is feeling because you have felt that way yourself.

Tragic (Tra-jic): Very sad. Usually used when talking about a death or an accident.

INDEX OF PAINTINGS

I hope you enjoyed this book. If you have time to post a brief review on Amazon that would be great. I always welcome helpful hints. Got to run - I've got a part in Fiona's adventure story... "What *do* you do in a Drawing Room?" Bye for now! Amber xx

Free activities to accompany this book can be found on the 'SMART READS for Kids' web pages at: www.theportraitplace.co.uk

Made in the USA
Middletown, DE
16 December 2017